M

THE SAINTE CHAPELLE

Photographs by the author
Translated by Angela Moyon

ÉDITIONS OUEST-FRANCE
13, rue du Breil, Rennes

A perfect example of 13th-century French architecture

The Sainte-Chapelle occupies a very special place among the monuments of Paris. Is it because of the magic of its stained glass windows, the prestige enjoyed by St. Louis, or the holiness of the relics for which it was built? Perhaps for all three reasons. Whatever the truth of the matter, there have always been large numbers of visitors to admire « one of the most beautiful residences of paradise », as a 14th-century theologian put it.

The Sainte-Chapelle was to be perfect; St. Louis wished it to be so. And it is indeed the creation of a king who not only showed respect for his duty but who was also proud of authority. This was a king who wanted to confirm his preeminence over a number of turbulent feudal lords by building within his palace the symbol of a power for which he was answerable to God alone. It was also the creation of a highly-active saint who believed that doing his job as king was a means of serving the Lord. He was a saint with a faith that was both luminous and tranquil, a saint who was happy to be able to create a wonderful reliquary that was worthy of prestigious relics reminding believers of Christ's existence and suffering on earth. Finally, the chapel was the work of a man who appreciated life and whose behaviour was never excessive, a man who found the joy of living in family affection and the loyalty of friends. King Louis ordered a building in line with the times that would provide him with the assurance of his mission on earth.

The Sainte-Chapelle is perfect, too, as far as the story of its construction is concerned. In the 13th Century, Gothic architecture had reached its peak, gracefully allying stability, lightness, and beauty. It was one of those fortunate periods when architecture reaches a sort of equilibrium, or a triumphant plenitude. There was a deep-seated harmony between the hierachical feudal society then in its heyday and the orderliness of the stones in a building that is crowned with fleurs-de-lys and bears a Cross, the symbols of royalty and the Church.

The angel on the chevet, a figure almost ten feet high holding a Cross above the town. In the past, a mechanism made it revolve on the hour. The masks decorating the base are portraits of the craftsmen who worked under Lassus to restore the chapel.

The holy relics of Christ's Passion leave Byzantium for Paris

At the beginning of the 13th Century, the Crusaders took Byzantium and founded a Roman Empire which was to last a mere fifty years. Hard-pressed by the Bulgarians, Turks and Greeks, Emperor Baudoin II of Courtenay had lost all power except in his capital city. In order to acquire funds, he placed in the custody of Venitian pawnbrokers the most precious of all relics — the Crown of Thorns. Then he set off for Europe in the hope of finding help and, perhaps, of promoting a new crusade. In 1237, he arrived in Paris where he met King Louis IX. The French sovereign was not in favour of a military expedition. Firstly, France had internal problems of its own and secondly the city of Jerusalem had been recaptured in 1229 by the Emperor of the Western World, Frederick II. The young king could not see any need for a crusade whose main aim was not the defence of the holy city. On the other hand, he was quite willing to purchase the relics under distraint in Venice. Negotiations lasted for two years. Although the king was anxious to bring his country the protection that the presence of such distinguished relics could provide, he was also determined to take every precaution with regard to guarantees of authenticity. Finally, for the sum of 135,000 livres, an astronomical figure in its day, the Holy Crown was brought to France by two Dominican friars. The King, his brother Robert, and their mother, Queen Blanche of Castille, went to meet them at Villeneuve-L'Archevêque. On 18th August 1239, the Crown of Thorns arrived in Paris and was placed in the chapel of Saint-Nicolas de la Cité. Two years later, Baudouin II sold the King of France more relics from Christ's Passion, in particular a large section of the True Cross. It was then that Louis IX had the idea of building within the palace a monument that was to be a veritable reliquary worthy of these precious relics, a chapel with an interior better-suited to the purpose than in St. Nicolas which had been built in the previous century.

The legend of the anonymous architect

When they learnt that the King of France wanted to have a new chapel built in his palace, a large number of architects set off from all over Europe to present their projects. One of them had drawn plans that he considered as perfect. Now, on his way, he met up with a colleague. When they stopped for the night, each showed the other his sketches. The first architect realised with no little bitterness that his design was far inferior to his companion's. He went mad with jealousy, murdered his rival and burnt his plans.

A few days later, he arrived in Paris. Every time he tried to enter the King's palace, however, a mysterious force prevented him from crossing the threshold. In desperation, he turned to drink. One

It is said to have been Louis XII, whose initial features on the balustrade, who restored the small **chapel** between the two buttresses on the south front. Its decoration is reminiscent of late 14th-century work. Below it was a door which was walled up in the 19th Century.

evening a young Dominican friar picked him up in the gutter and comforted him. The unhappy man confessed his crime and, on the friar's advice, entered holy orders. Several months passed in an atmosphere of calm and prayer. One day the architect, by then a novice, met a pastrycook's son who dreamt of creating real buildings instead of the sweetmeat architecture his father made. The novice grew fond of the young man called Pierre and taught him the secrets of his art. Moreover, he learnt that the King had seen numerous projects but that he had not considered any of them to be worthy of a chapel destined to house such very sacred relics.

The architect went to the monastery in search of the Dominican who had taken pity on him. He described young Pierre to him in glowing terms and asked permission for the young man to show the King his original designs, without revealing the architect's name. He then added, «If my design finds royal favour, Pierre will have an opportunity of taking up a profession for which he is eminently suited and I shall at last be at peace.» The Dominican gave his consent and the pastrycook's son was given an audience with King Louis. The sovereign was delighted with the plans that were presented to him but expressed amazement that such detailed work had been brought by somebody so young. Pierre told him the truth — the project was the work of an architect who wished to remain anonymous but, with God's help, he would be quite able to take charge of the construction himself. The King accepted. And so it was that the Sainte-Chapelle was built without anybody ever knowing the name of its designer. As to the Dominican in the story, he was called Thomas Aquinas.

It is a fine legend, but the story is quite untrue. Pierre de Montreuil was a great architect who worked on Saint-Denis, Saint-Germain-des-Prés and Notre-Dame. Unfortunately, in 1240, he was already middle-aged and he enjoyed the King's favour. Some authors have put his name forward, although there is no written evidence for this. We must therefore resign ourselves to never knowing the name of the architect who designed this work of art.

From 1242 to 1248 — the building of the Sainte-Chapelle

Work got underway rapidly. In 1246, Louis IX founded a college of Canons. Two years later, the building work was completed. It had cost the Crown 40,000 livres. It was consecrated on 26th April 1248, the papal Legate Eudes de Châteauroux officiating in the upper chapel, and Pierre Berruyer, Bishop of Bourges, in the lower chapel. Several months later, the King embarked at Aigues-Mortes for the Sixth Crusade. Before setting off, he provided sufficient funds for the upkeep of the Sainte-Chapelle, thereby fulfilling civil and religious duties. Churchwardens were given responsibility for the relics and the upkeep of the monument, while Canons ensured the continuance of the religious ceremonies. With the important

The Holy Relics arriving in Sens. St.Louis and Robert of Artois are bearing the stretcher on which the relics have been placed. Before them is the gateway into the town. At their feet is a small figure on his knees.

functions ascribed to him, the prime dignitary was a powerful person at Court. He changed titles several times — Master Chaplain, Master Governor,Treasurer, Arch-chaplain and even, during the reign of François I, Pope of the Sainte-Chapelle!

The relics housed in the chapel were many and various. In addition to the Crown of Thorns and a piece of the True Cross, there were fragments of the Holy Lance, of the Holy Sponge, and of Christ's Mantel and Shroud. Texts mention the Precious Blood, the milk and hair of the Virgin Mary, part of St. John the Baptist's skull, the Rod of Moses, and many other objects from both Testaments. Thereafter, new relics were added to the original list. In particular, a magnificent reliquary was placed in the chapel in 1306 containing the head of St.Louis who had been canonised in 1299.

On Good Friday every year, the relics became the object of devotion of the faithful, and the sick (especially epileptics) were permitted to touch them. Usually, they were placed in a large richly-decorated reliquary on a dais in the centre of the chancel, a reliquary for which the king kept the key and which he showed personally to any sovereign visiting Paris. Small pieces of these relics were given away by successive monarchs. Thus it was that Charles V gave his brother-in-law Emperor Charles IV of Bohemia a Thorn, while his brother the Duke of Berry received a piece of the True Cross.

From St. Louis to Louis XVI — five centuries of work

Some years after the building was completed, the «Trésor-des-Chartes» was added onto the north side. This small two-storey building, a sort of scale model of the Sainte-Chapelle, was used as the sacristy and archives. When, in 1383, the framework for the steeple proved to have rotted, it was replaced by a new wooden construction covered with lead designed by the Master Carpenter Robert Fouchier.

Numerous ceremonies were held in the Sainte-Chapelle, the most important being the coronation of Queen Mary, Philip the Bold's second wife, in 1275, and the crowning of Isabeau of Bavaria, Charles-VI's wife, in 1389.

In the 15th Century, when tastes had changed, several clockwork objects were made in order to add interest to the services. During the Whitsun Mass, for example, an angel came down from the roof bringing water to the celebrant for the lavabo. In 1484, young Charles VII was filled with such wonder at this theatrical machinery that he had it used on the two following Sundays. This particular monarch restored the building and, more importantly, had the rose window in the west wall rebuilt between 1490 and 1495. Louis XII had a large staircase added along the south wall giving direct access from the courtyard to the upper chapel, while still on the south side he had the external decoration repeated on a small oratory built inthe 14th century so that the sovereign could follow the Mass without being seen.

The rose window in the west gable end with its vigorous Flamboyant Gothic ribs was built in the late 15th Century, during the reign of Charles VIII whose monogram is included in one of the windows.

During the reign of Henri II, the choir-screen was replaced by a carved wooden roodscreen with a door flanked by two altars. The reredos behind these altars were decorated with enamelwork made in 1553 by Léonard Limousin after drawings ascribed to Primaticcio. Both these enamels are now in the Louvre. There was also an organ, in front of the west rose window; the last organist was François Couperin.

Several catastrophes befell the monument from the 17th Century onwards. In 1630, the roof and steeple caught fire. They were not restored until 1671, and the new steeple lacked the grace of its predecessors. During the winter of 1689-1690, the Seine burst its banks, causing unusually bad flooding. Water poured into the lower chapel and the stained glass windows were destroyed. Finally, in 1776, another fire ruined part of the Law Courts. They were rebuilt to entirely new designs and,in order to create a symmetrical layout in the May Courtyard, the « Trésor-des-Chartes » was demolished to make way for the present building which unfortunately darkens the lights in the north windows in the upper chapel.

After the damage of the Revolution, the architect Lassus begins restoration work

As a symbol of royalty whose decoration it bore, the Sainte-Chapelle seemed doomed to suffer damage on a scale far worse than in other churches during the Revolution. Yet although it was not demolished, it was very badly damaged. All the furnishings, the choirstalls, and the roodscreens were removed.The organ was taken to Saint-Germain-L'Auxerrois. All the royal insignia were destroyed, and the steeple was taken down. The reliquaries were sent to the Mint, and the relics dispersed. What could be saved is now part of Notre-Dame's treasure. Other objects are now kept in the National Library, either in the Medals Department, or in the Manuscripts Section.

The building itself suffered badly. The tympana were hammered clean as were any parts of the building bearing crowns and fleurs-de-lys. However, Lenoir managed to save most of the statues which were taken to the Museum of French Monuments. The upper chapel was first turned into a club room then, from 1803 onwards, into the legal archives department. The stained glass windows were removed up to a height of 6 1/2 ft. to allow for the installation of shelving. Some of these windows were sold off, mainly in England.

At the 1836 exhibition, the architect Lassus showed a project for the monument's restoration and his work attracted considerable attention. Yet it took another ten years for a government commission to order him to give the Sainte-Chapelle back all its original splendour, working first with Duban and then on his own. When he died in 1857, Lassus had completed a quite outstan-

This **statue of St.Louis** holds a double-barred Cross. This type of Cross was then known as a Greek, or overseas, Cross because it was the symbol of the True Cross. Later it was called the Cross of Anjou, before being renamed Cross of Lorraine.

ding piece of restoration work. His name has remained linked to the building, especially to the steeple which is a masterpiece of carpentry. The work was not finished until 1867 under the direction of the architect Boeswillwald.

The Sainte-Chapelle — a marvel of Gothic architecture at its very best

The Sainte-Chapelle is one of a number of private chapels built in the residences of high-ranking people. They have two storeys. The upper chapel was reserved for his Lordship and was on the same level as his apartments, while the lower church was for his servants' use. Among these two-storey chapels, though, the Sainte-Chapelle is unique for its size and its exceptional decoration. Unfortunately, surrounded as it is by mediocre buildings, it cannot be seen to its best advantage. Yet it is an austere, concise building of elegant proportions. A single aisle with four spans leads to a seven-sided chevet. At the west end, a two-storey porch affords protection for the doors into the chapels while two turrets contain service stairs. The design of the building is emphasised by powerful buttresses with stark ribs rising from a solid bare basement up to the luminous windows in the upper chapel. Outside, the decorative features are concentrated on the upper section — gables ornamented with crochets connect the buttresses topped by pinnacles in the shape of pyramids with tragic-faced gargoyles at their base. Further up, on small turrets, are stone cones carved with crowns of thorns: the turrets flank the gable end on top of which stands a fleur-de-lys. The steeply-sloping lead roof has an openwork ridge dominated at the east end by an angel facing Notre-Dame. Finally, above all this decoration in stone and lead is the steeple. At 107 feet, this cedarwood masterpiece created by the Master Carpenter Bellu was designed using old documents illustrating the slim 15th-century steeple. The result is wonderfully ethereal; it rests on an octagonal base decorated with statues of the twelve Apostles to whom the sculptor Geoffroy Dechaume gave the features of Lassus and the main craftsmen who worked on the restoration of the monument.

The lower chapel, reserved for the royal servants

It was dedicated to the Virgin Mary whose statue stands in front of the pier in the doorway while on the tympanum there is a carving of her coronation. In order to avoid giving this chapel the appearance of a crypt (its vaulted roof is very low), short pillars with capitals bearing crochets stand at each end of the

From the top of the steeple, the view stretches down the Seine as far as the Louvre. Among the sculptures decorating the pinnacle above one of the staircase turrets is a crown of thorns.

arches in the centre aisle, separating it from the narrow side aisles which are further divided by small flying buttresses. The walls are decorated with three-lobed arcading and twelve medallions ornamented with cabochons and small pieces of glass representing the Apostles. A painting of a star-studded sky decorates the vaulting while on the pillars the fleurs-de-lys of France on an azure background alternate with the towers of Castille on a red background in honour of St.Louis' mother. The paintings were restored in the 19th Century, as were the stained glass windows which had been destroyed by the 1690 flood. In the floor are a large number of tombstones, unfortunately all very worn. They used to cover the graves of treasurers and canons. Boileau was buried among them. The Academician, whose tomb is now in Saint-Germain-des-Prés,was particularly well-known for his poem «Lutrin» (Lectern), which depicted in humourous style a court case opposing the cantor of the Sainte-Chapelle and its treasurer over a period of several years, arising from the placing of the said piece of furniture.

The upper chapel, the chapel of the Kings of France

It was built to house the relics of Christ's Passion. A statue of Christ decorates the pier on the doorway while the tympanum depicts the Last Judgement and the lintel bears carvings of the Resurrection of the Dead. Twenty small bas-reliefs on the jambs illustrate scenes from Genesis. They include the Creation, Adam and Eve, and the story of Noah. All these carvings are 19th-century copies.

The interior is the most sumptuous part of the building. When visitors step out of the small dark winding staircase,they are first of all struck by the dazzling light which gives the nave a quite unreal appearance. In this almost magical atmosphere, mediaeval Christians felt the presence of God and all miracles became possible. Here Gothic architecture is expressed with a maximum of effect. The star-studded vaulting seems to be floating above the stained glass windows whose slim mullions provide a framework that is apparently too light. The magnificence of the windows makes visitors forget the massive stone base decorated with three-lobed arcading over thin colonettes. A stone bench runs round the walls. It stands back from the arcading on both sides of the third arch forming a recess which is traditionally said to have been the king and queen's place. In the following arch on the south side is a small enclosed shrine built in the reign of Louis XI from which the king could follow the service through a window cut sideways into the wall.

The altar used to stand at the entrance to the apse. Behind it is the dais on which the relics were placed on public view. Connected to the side walls by a screen of traceried arcading, it is supported by ogi-

It is difficult to know what to admire most — the airiness of the architecture or the shimmer of the stained glass windows. It is perhaps rather more the fine balance of both these features which makes the **upper chapel** a marvel of Gothic architecture. (Photo by Nicolas Fediaevsky).

Overleaf:

The lower chapel was reserved for the palace servants. The architect found an elegant solution to the problem of how to decrease the span of the arches — he incorporated slim colonettes and light inner buttresses. (Photo by Nicolas Fediaevsky)

val arches. Above it is a gilded wooden canopy. It was accessible from two small staircases, also made of gilded wood. Only the left-hand staircase is original.

Behind the main front, beneath the rose window and the gallery which lead to the organ that no longer exists, three large arches bear barely-visible paintings representing Christ and the prophets. Finally, the stone flags are incrusted with coloured mastic to a design by Boeswillwald.

A rich and varied set of carvings

Backing onto the engaged pillars marking the arches, the statues of the twelve Apostles bear the crosses from the consecration of the chapel. These statues are the most important carvings in the upper chapel, for at least half of them are original. Lenoir had them removed in 1797. Two of them were broken when being transported elsewhere. Thereafter, when the Museum of French Monuments was closed down, the statues were dispersed, some going to Saint-Denis, others to the Mont-Valérien and one to the church in Créteil. In 1844, they were collected up again but only six of them were in sufficiently good condition to warrant their being put back in their original position even though two of them were headless. The others were replaced by copies and the originals were stored in the Cluny Museum. The four original statues decorate the supports for the fourth arch, the one just in front of the apse.

These apostles are magnificent pieces of work belonging to two different styles. The first group comprises the westernmost statues, probably dating from St.Louis' reign. They give an impression of tranquillity and serenity. The clothes are gently draped round the figures, the folds are perfect, the fine features on the faces are slightly emphasised and all the statues have flat curly hair. The influence of the Fine God on the central pillar in Amiens Cathedral is very much in evidence here. The second group comprising the eastern statues might be later, doubtless from the reign of Philip the Fair. There is a very marked contrast between the two groups. Here, the volume is suggested by stiff broken folds which catch the light. The faces with their clear-cut features are made less austere by their smiles, while the hair and beards add a touch of lightness that increases the life-like expressions on the faces. All this is reminiscent of the Golden Virgin portal at the south end of the transept in Amiens Cathedral.

The carvings, though, do not consist solely of statues. First of all, there is the excellent quality of the capitals on the colonettes. Numbering approximately one hundred, they are all different in design. Although some of them are stylised, most of them include natural-looking foliage freely placed around the basket. All types of plantlife are represented — oaks, holly, ivy, vines, fig trees, even a rose tree in bloom, not forgetting wild flowers like renunculas, violets and hemlock.

Elsewhere, in the squinches, angels are shown spreading their wings. Others are seen converging on a bust of Christ above the recesses in the third arch. It is all reminiscent of the art of the goldsmith and ivory-carver. The wealth of decoration, often in miniature, is a sure indication that the Sainte-Chapelle was treated as a veritable reliquary.

The Sainte-Chapelle contains some one hundred **capitals**, all of them different, but with a decoration of foliage treated with great realism. Visitors can see all the flora of France represented on them and may even notice a lizard or a bird beneath the leaves.

The paintings — a model of 19th-century restoration

The entire interior of the chapel is covered with paintings which blend in with the stained glass windows. Restored in the 19th Century, the multicoloured artwork was based on traces of the original paintings which had survived up to the time of the restoration,except for the back of the main facade which is a creation of Steinheil's and in doubtful taste. The colonettes and ribs are decorated with twirls of foliage or a variety of other swirled motifs. The painting on the walls imitates the decorated drapes of animals which were stencilled into place. The statues are painted blue and gold, the edge of the robes being further enriched with small pieces of glass while the crosses of the consecration stand out against circular glass bases. Touches of gold add a sumptuous brilliance to this dazzling decor.

In the forty-two quadrilobes above the arcading on the side walls are medallions decorated in the same fashion as the statues of the Apostles in the lower chapel. Unfortunately, most of them have been damaged. The figures are painted onto glass and stucco backgrounds so that the plaques look like enamelwork. When the light is reflected in them, they resemble the stained glass windows above them. Beside the martyrdom of St.Sebastian, St.Hippolytus and St.John, is the murder of St.Thomas a Becket. Nor are St.Denis, the first Bishop of Paris, St.Lawrence and St.Stephen forgotten.

The windows — a Bible in colour and light

The stained glass windows have to be treated separately; it is the windows which have brought the Sainte-Chapelle its renown. They form one of the most complete series of mediaeval art anywhere in the world. In the early years of the 13th Century, the workshop in Chartres had enormous influence with its very elaborate style. The artist had perfect mastery over the interplay of colours, skilfully separating them in order to avoid the clash of bright colours on more muted shades. Paris became the centre of stained glass c.1240. Its manufacture was then less delicate. Production took place on a large scale, calling for processes that might be described as industrial. The work on the edging in particular is less meticulous and the same motif is repeated ad infinitum. Elsewhere on the windows, there is no longer any separation between blues and reds and the brightness of the one overwhelms the other. It results in a violet hue that was much appreciated in its day. Hence the saying that connoisseurs liked to see in their glass «wine the colour of the windows in the Sainte-Chapelle». Although these dazzling backgrounds bring a certain unity to the windows, the individual scenes are difficult to make out. Moreover, the metal framework no longer has the simple shape it had in Chartres glass; it forms medallions of varying designs

Of all the statues of the Apostles in the upper chapel, the one of St.James, son of Alphaeus, is one of the most pleasing. The technique used in the drape of the cloth emphasising the light and shade, and the carving on the face which is both grave and highly-expressive, are typical of mid 13th-century art. (Photo by Nicolas Fediaevsky).

which add to the decoration. It would seem, indeed, that the artists were particularly concerned to create a sort of mosaic of colour within an overall pattern and that they paid little heed to making visible the small pictures placed far away from the naked eye. According to Professor Louis Grodecki, who is considered to be an authority on such matters, three different workshops were involved in the Sainte-Chapelle. The first one created the decoration on the north side and in the apse, while the other two shared responsibility for the south side. The differences exist in the design but they are far from obvious to uninformed visitors.

In the Sainte-Chapelle, the side windows comprise four lights, whereas the ones in the apse have only two. There are three multilobed rose windows above them. Each window deals with one particular topic, except for the three in the chancel on which each light should be read separately. The Old Testament is developed mainly on the side windows. Starting at the first arch at the north end, they depict Genesis, Exodus, the story of Joshua, the Books of Judges and Isaiah, then on the south side the stories of Daniel, Ezekial, Jeremiah, Tobiah, Judith and Job, Esther and finally the Book of Kings. To end with, in the first arch at the south end is the story of the relics themselves. The series is broken at the chevet by the Passion in line with the nave, flanked by a Rod of Jesse, the life of St.John the Evangelist, and the childhood of Christ on one side, and by the life of St.John the Baptist on the other side.

The west rose window was rebuilt at the end of the 15th Century. The windows date from this same period and are quite different both in style and colour. They provide a faithful illustration of the story of the Apocalypse and it is more than likely that the 13th-century window dealt with this same theme.

In Vincennes, Saint-Germain-en-Laye and Saint-Germer-de-Fly are buildings whose architecture has many points in common with the Sainte-Chapelle. None of them, however, provokes such an émotional feeling as the one aroused by St.Louis' chapel. The elegant structure of the monument is forgotten when visitors come face-to-face with the splendour of the stained glass windows that make up its decoration. Built to house the most moving of all relics for a Christian, this masterpiece of Gothic architecture is an act of faith which still cannot leave anybody cold.

DETAILS OF THE STATUES AND WINDOWS

The statues of the Apostles:

1 — St.John (modern)
2 —
3 — unidentified (modern)
4 — St.James, the son of Alphaeus (original)
5 — Unidentified (original)
6 — St.Peter (original, head replaced)
7 — St.Paul (modern)
8 — Unidentified (original)
9 — St.James, the brother of John (original)
10 — Unidentified (original, head replaced) replaced)
11 — St. Bartholomew (modern)
12 — Unidentified (modern)

Identification of the windows

Each window should be read from left to right and from bottom to top. The identification of the various scenes is based on the indications provided by Mr. Louis Grodecki in his work on the Sainte-Chapelle published by the National Historic Monuments Dept. in 1959.

The disciples in Emmaus. The three figures are shown sitting at a table. Christ is breaking the bread and it is this gesture which reveals His identity to the disciples. A wisp of cloud isolates Christ who will soon leave them on their own. (St.Luke's Gospel, Chap.24, v.30).

Window A — Genesis

The windows were badly damaged during the 16th Century when the organ was installed and during the 18th Century during work on the Law Courts. Of the 86 scenes depicted here, only seven are more or less authentic.

— The creation of the world (6 scenes).
— The creation of man and original sin (8).
— Cain and Abel (3).
— The descendants of Adam (6).
— The story of Noah (9).
— The Tower of Babel (2).
— The story of Abraham (6).
— The story of Lot (3).
— The story of Isaac (14).
— The story of Jacob (7)
— The story of Joseph (11).
— Joseph and his brothers (8).
— The arrival of the Hebrews in Egypt (3 in the rose window).

Window B — Exodus.

This window may be considered as one of the best preserved of the series. Of the 121 scenes, 92 are original.

— The childhood of Moses (4 scenes).
— Moses in the desert and his wedding (9).
— God gives Moses the commandments (7).
— The plagues of Egypt (13).
— The Hebrews offend God (11).
— The Hebrews in the desert and the miracles of Moses (26).
— The battle against Amalek (4).
— The Golden Calf and the Tablets of the Law (18).
— Moses and Aaron (20).
— Joseph's wedding and death (9 scenes in the rose window).

Window C — Numbers

Of the 97 scenes depicted here, 70 are original. The panels in Twycross Church and Rouen Museum both come from this window.

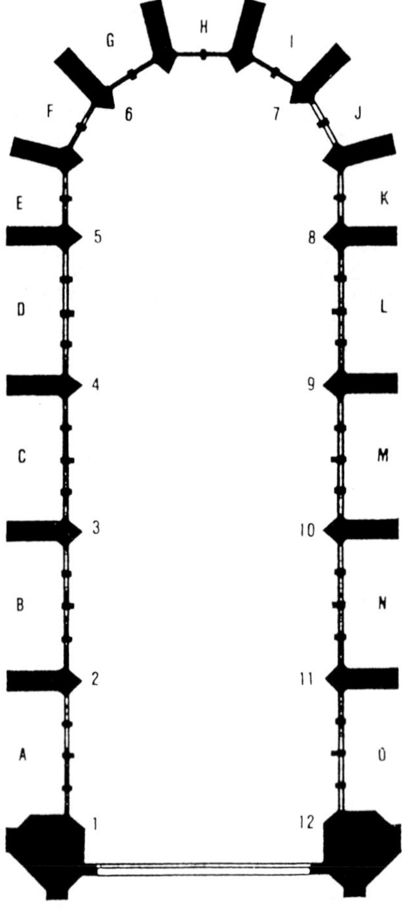

— God speaks through the Tabernacle (4 scenes).
— The coronation of the Princes of Israel (20).
— The impure are cast out and offerings are made (6).
— The service of the Tabernacle (7).
— Moses has problems with his people (11).

The Adoration of the Beast. A woman and an old man in a red cloak are shown kneeling before the Beast with seven heads (Apocalypse, Chap.13, vv.8-12).

— The Promised Land (9).
— War with Amalek (4).
— Moses and Aaron (13).
— The Hebrews enter Palestine (14).
— Miscellaneous (9 in the rose window).

Window D — Deuteronomy; Joshua.

Of the 65 scenes depicted here, 53 are original. This is one of the most beautiful of all the windows in the chapel. The design of the panels shows a rare unity and the blue tones are particularly luminous.

— Deuteronomy. The death of Moses (12 scenes).
— The fall of Jericho (18).
— The extermination of the Infidel; circumcision (6).
— War against the Amorites (8).
— Joshua's last battles (10).
— The death of Joshua (2).
— Ruth and Boaz (9 in the rose window).

Window E — Judges.

Of the 64 scenes depicted here, only 26 are original. This is due to the original proximity of the «Trésor-des-Chartes». Its demolition damaged the window.

— Ehud, Deborah, and the Moabites (6 scenes).
— Gideon's sacrifice (8).
— Gideon and the Midianites (10).
— Gideon crowned (4).
— The deaths of Gideon and Abimelech (4).
— The story of Jephthah (8).
— The birth and marriage of Samson (4).
— Samson's feats of strength (10).
— Samson and Delilah (4).
— Samson destroys the temple Dagon (6).

Window F — Isaiah (left light).

This window is pictorially interesting inasmuch as it includes numerous references to the Apocrypha. It is fairly well-preserved. Of the 24 scenes depicted on it, 18, are original.

— Isaiah and the Judges of Israel (5 scenes).
— The prophecies of Isaiah (6).
— Isaiah and Asaph (10).
— The torture of Isaiah (3).

Window F — Rod of Jesse (right light).

The subject is developed vertically on the central panels (18). Each of them is framed by figures of prophets (34) and angels (2). Of the 54 panels, 41 are original.

Above the sleeping figure of Jesse are David and Solomon, the 12 kings, and finally the Virgin Mary and Christ. The upper section shows the three doves representing the gifts of the Holy Spirit.

Window G — St.John the Evangelist (left light).

16 scenes including 9 originals, all dealing with the miracles of St. John.

— The saint is brought before Domitian.
— He is plunged into boiling oil.
— His journey to Patmos.
— He writes the Apocalypse.
— He changes leaves into gold.
— He brings two young people back to life (2).
— He causes the collapse of the temple of Diana.
— He drinks the poisoned cup.
— The conversion of Aristodemus.
— The pursuit of a thief.
— The death of St.John (2).

Young Tobiah and the angel. The angel is helping Tobiah who has met Sarah for the first time when she was introduced by her parents. It is a strange scene; the fiancés have turned their backs on each other. (Tobit, Chap.7, v.2).

Window G — The childhood of Christ (right light).

In this window, only the lower two panels are modern.

- The Annunciation and Visitation of the Virgin Mary.
- The Nativity and the Adoration of the Shepherds.
- The Three Wise men.
- The Circumcision.
- The massacre of the Innocents.
- The flight into Egypt.
- The fall of the graven images.

Window H — Christ's Passion.

A total of 42 scenes out of the 54 are original. This window, lying in line with the nave, depicts the Passion in the usual order without making any reference to the relics. It is considered to be the most outstanding window in the Sainte-Chapelle.

- Angels bearing the instruments of the Passion (4 scenes).
- The Last Supper.
- The kiss of Judas.
- The judgement of Christ (8).
- Christ is scourged and crowned with thorns (2).
- The sentencing of Christ (6).
- Jesus carrying the Cross (2).
- The Crucifixion.
- Christ is brought down from the Cross.
- Christ is laid in the tomb (9).
- The Resurrection (9).
- The disciples in Emmaus (2).
- Angels bearing incense (4).
- Pentecost (4).

Window I — St. John the Baptist (left light).

Of the 16 panels, 10 are original.

- The birth of St.John (5 scenes).
- St.John preaching and the Baptism of Christ (6).
- The death of St.John (5).

Window I — The story of Daniel (right light).

Of the 15 scenes, 12 are original.

- Daniel and Nebuchadnezzar (5 scenes).
- Nebuchadnezzar's dream (3).
- Belshazzar's feast and his death (2).
- Daniel in the den of lions (5).

Window J — Ezekial.

Of the 28 scenes on this window, 17 are original. The colours are very vivid because of the abundance of yellow glass.

The main themes are the prophet's visions. They proved to be of major importance for the study of theology. The most famous panels depict the vision of the Tetramorphe and Ezekial coming upon the idolaters (3rd and 6th scenes in the left light).

Window K — Jeremiah (left light).

Of the 25 scenes depicted here, 19 are original. It is fairly rare to see the prophecies of Jeremiah treated in such depth. Some of the original panels are now in London.

- God sanctifies Jeremiah (2 scenes).
- Jeremiah's vision (2).
- God and Jeremiah (2).
- Jeremiah in the potter's workshop (3).
- Jeremiah and Baruch in prison (5).
- The wrath of God (6).
- A new vision and the destruction of Jerusalem (5).

Window K — Tobiah (right light).

This story, which is told in a series of 25 scenes including 16 originals, is developed in a quite exceptional manner.

- The piety and charity of the aged

The Angel of the Abyss, holding a golden sceptre in his hand, rides before a horde of locusts on a horse with a man's head. (Apocalypse, Chap.9, v.11).

Tobiah (2 scenes).
- The birth of his son (2).
- Tobiah in captivity (3).
- Tobiah and Sennacherib (3).
- Tobiah becomes blind.
- The journey of the young Tobiah (4).
- The marriage of Tobiah and Sarah (7).

Window L — Judith and Job.

Of the 56 scenes depicted here, only 32 are original. The two stories are told one above the other, Judith's story (40) being related in the lower section.

- Holopherne enters the campaign (8 scenes).
- The Israelites prepare to put up resistance (8).
- Holopherne besieges Bethulie (3).
- Judith prepares her project (5).
- The meeting of Judith and Holopherne (4).
- Holopherne's feast and death (3).
- The besieged people launch an attack (4).
- Judith's triumph and death (5).
- Job and his sons (2).
- Job's first tribulations (10).
- Job on the compost heap (4).
- The triumph of Job (in the rose window).

Window M — Esther.

Of the 120 scenes depicted here, 91 are original. This window was already in very poor condition in 1848, moreover the paint in the grisaille has aged very badly. In order to fill one hundred panels with the story of Esther which is one of the shortest in the Bible, the artist had to repeat certain scenes and illustrate episodes of minor importance.

- Ahasuerus' feast (4 scenes).
- The coronation of Esther (8).
- Mordecai discovers the plot (5).
- Esther reveals the plot (5).
- The guilty are executed (8).
- Haman is named governor (9).
- Conflict between Haman and Mordecai (7).
- Esther before Ahasuerus (12).
- Esther's feast (8).
- The triumph of Mordecai (6).
- Esther — the second feast (9).
- The execution of Haman (8).
- Ahasuerus and Mordecai (6).
- The Jews take their revenge (8).
- The glory of Mordecai (6).
- The Hebrews render thanks (in the rose window).

Window N — The Book of Kings.

Of the 121 scenes depicted here, 86 are original but in many cases have undergone major restoration. The pictorial details often lack precision. This window is of limited interest.

- The victory of the Philistines (6 scenes).
- The Ark of the Covenant returns to Israel (4).
- Saul and Samuel (7).
- David and Goliath (4).
- David defeats the Philistines (4).
- David flees (8).
- David and Achimelech (6).
- David and Abigail (3).
- The fight between Saul and David (15).
- David attacks Amalek (4).
- The death of Saul (7).
- The coronation of David (10).
- David and Bathsheba (3).
- The death of David (3).
- Eli and Ahab (7).
- The death of Jezebel (4).
- Atalia and Joas (5).
- Pillaging and fire in the Temple (4).
- Scenes from the story of Solomon (9 in the rose window).

Armed with a bow, **the First Horseman of the Apocalypse** is shown riding a grey. This is one of the best-preserved panels in the rose window. (Apocalypse, Chap.6, v.2).

Window O — The story of the relics.

This window is one of the least well-preserved in the chapel. Of the 67 scenes depicted, only 26 are original. They are very interesting from a pictorial point of view. First of all, the illustration shows the Discovery of the True Cross as in the Golden Legend, then its purchase and the transport of the relics of Christ's Passion.

— Helen discovers the True Cross and the nails (16 scenes).
— Khosro ransacks Jerusalem (3).
— The victory of Heraclius (9).
— The shipment of the relics (5).
— St.Louis carrying the relics (9).
— The relics in Paris (4).
— The purchase of more relics (4).
— The removal of the relics (6).
— The building and consecration of the Sainte-Chapelle (4).
— The adoration of the relics (7 in the rose window).

The rose window — The Apocalypse.

This window is fairly well-preserved, and is a brilliant piece of work in which the dominant colours are green and yellow. Around a multilobed circle showing St.John prostrate at the feet of Christ who is sitting on a rainbow, is a story which should be read clockwise starting from the top in three concentric sections. The design, though, of the panels makes it difficult to decipher. The figure of Charles VIII provides absolute confirmation of its date.

Front cover :
The Sainte-Chapelle.

Back cover :
The Christ of the Apocalypse. In accordance with the description given by St.John who is prostrate at His feet, Christ is seated on a rainbow and is clenching a sword between His teeth. He is surrounded by the seven candelabras and stars. (Apocalypse, Chap.1, vv.12-17).

 - I.S.B.N. 2 7373.1617.0 - Dépôt légal : avril 1994 - N° d'éditeur : 3006.01.09.04.94
Imprimerie Raynard, La Guerche-de-Bretagne (35).